The Admissions Edge

Your Path to College

Starting Early, Staying Strategic, and Finishing Confident
How to Find a School That Truly Fits

By Colleen Hart

This book is intended for informational and educational purposes only. The author does not guarantee any specific outcome related to college admissions decisions. Admissions policies, requirements, and practices may change, and readers are encouraged to verify information directly with colleges and universities.

ISBN: 979-8-218-91782-1

Printed in the United States of America

To my daughters, Anna and Jenna, whose own college journeys helped shape my perspective, informed the stories shared here, and deepened my commitment to helping students find schools where they can truly thrive.

And to my husband, Greg, who listened when I shared my hope of pursuing something meaningful, and who has quietly supported and encouraged me every step of the way.

Thank you

Table of Contents

Introduction

Why This Book Exists

The college admissions process can feel overwhelming, confusing, and emotionally charged for both students and parents. This book was written to replace stress with clarity and to turn a chaotic process into a thoughtful, manageable journey.

I have been married for over 30 years and I'm now a proud mother of two adult daughters. Like many parents, I've experienced the college journey both professionally and personally, having stood on both sides of the admissions desk. I understand the excitement, the pressure, the uncertainty, and the deeply emotional nature of this transition, not just as an educator, but as a parent.

Education has been the foundation of my entire adult life. As an undergraduate at the University of Pittsburgh, I majored in English Literature and immediately went on to earn my Master of Arts in Teaching (MAT) degree. I taught in both private and public education before moving to Georgia in 2011, where I continued to coach, tutor, and teach while raising our two daughters with my husband.

After several years of pro bono editing student college essays, I transitioned into private college consulting and officially began working as an Independent Educational Consultant (IEC).

Each year, I visit colleges and universities, attend professional conferences, participate in professional and colleague administered webinars, and enroll in continuing education courses. I am a Professional Member of the Independent Educational Consultants Association (IECA), a designation that requires at least three years of counseling or admissions experience, a master's degree, and a demonstrated history of visiting 25–50 college campuses within the past five years. Professional Members must also submit an application, provide professional references, and agree to abide by the Principles of Good Practice.

I am also a member of the Southern Association for College Admissions Counseling (SACAC). In addition, I hold several professional certificates, including College Admissions Ethics, Fundamentals in Financial Aid, Emerging Leaders Program Professional, and Transitioning to Private Practice, issued by the National Association for College Admission Counseling (NACAC).

My focus is to guide students through the college application process in a supportive and stress-free environment. We cooperatively work on essays, resumes, the Common Application, interview preparation, course selection, extracurricular planning, and the creation of thoughtful college lists.

Using a step-by-step framework, I help students identify their ideal college or university fit. Together, we build applications using each student's authentic voice to help them find the school where they will thrive academically, socially, emotionally, and professionally.

How to Use This Book

The Admissions Edge, Your Path to College is designed to be read from start to finish, but it also works as a guide you can return to whenever you need direction. The book follows the same path families experience in real life, from early planning to final decisions. So, you can step in wherever you are and find what matters most right now.

With that perspective in mind, the next question becomes how to navigate this book in a way that best supports where you are right now in the process.

If You Are Just Getting Started

Begin with **Part I and II: Strategy, Risk & Letting Go and Building the Foundation**. These chapters explain why hiring an IEC strategically improves your child's college application outcomes. They introduce what truly drives college admissions success, how to start making smart choices long before applications are due, and when it's time for parents to move into the passenger seat.

If You Are in Junior or Senior Year

Move into **Part III: The Timeline Years**, which walks you through how junior and senior year unfold. Understanding what matters when and why will immediately lower anxiety and help to avoid last-minute scrambling.

If You Are Working on Applications Right Now

Use **Part IV through Part VI: Reading Signals, Constructing Your List and Strengthening Your Application** as your playbook. These chapters walk you through the detailed pieces that most directly impact admissions decisions:

- Green light, yellow light and red-light schools

- ACT/SAT Timing, Timing and More Timing
- GPA, What Courses and Why They Matter
- Growth Over Perfection
- When it's Time for Students to Move from the Passenger Seat to Taking the Wheel
- Financial Figures
- Why Being on Campus Matters
- EA, ED, RD Explained
- Avoiding Common Mistakes
- Choosing Meaningful Activities
- Creating a Strong Student Resume
- Writing Personal and Supplemental Essays
- The Ever-Evolving AI

Many families move through these chapters slowly, reading one, applying what they've learned, then returning when they're ready for the next step.

If You Are Waiting on Decisions or if Your Path is Choosing an Alternate Route

Part VII and VIII: Decisions and Outcomes and When the Path Isn't Straight is here for the most emotional stage of the process. Whether you are celebrating acceptances, navigating deferrals, facing rejection, considering transfer options, community or junior colleges, or a gap year, these chapters will help you stay grounded and focused on what comes next, not just what just happened.

Resource Pages

I've included resource pages designed to be used as tools for creating your own **Toolbox**. These pages include practical items such as:

- Essay Guidance
- College Terminology
- College and University Visit Questions

- College List Checklists
- Application Burnout
- A Full Admissions Roadmap

These pages are meant to be used, revisited, and relied on as you move through your own college application process.

Parents and Students: Read This Together!

Some chapters speak more directly to students. Others speak to parents. Many invite conversations.

This book works best when it becomes a shared guide, helping families communicate clearly, plan intentionally, and stay aligned during a time that can otherwise feel uncertain.

One Final Thought

There is no single "path" to take through college admissions. But there is a thoughtful, intentional route. I recommend before diving into timelines, lists, and applications, it's important to understand the mindset that drives successful admissions decisions.

Use this book to slow down when you need to, regain clarity when things feel overwhelming, and stay focused on what truly matters: finding a college where you will grow, belong, and thrive.

Part I: Strategy, Risk, & Letting Go

1

Reducing Risk and Maximizing Opportunity in Admissions

At the end of every application cycle, colleges and universities release their academic data through the Common Data Set (CDS). This information outlines the academic profile of admitted students, average GPA, test scores, course rigor, extracurricular engagement, and increasingly, insights into shifting admissions priorities. In many ways, colleges are showing families what has worked and what they value most each year.

However, while this information is publicly available, interpreting it accurately, and applying it strategically to an individual student is far from simple. Data without context can be misleading. This is where my role as an Independent Educational Consultant (IEC) becomes both practical and valuable. I do my best to take complex, often overwhelming data and translate it into a clear, organized, and actionable plan for both parents and students. Transparency is central to my approach, which helps keep stress low and expectations realistic throughout the process.

Once families understand how admissions data works, a natural question follows: **Who helps interpret it correctly?**

Knowing the numbers is one thing. Knowing how to apply them to a real student, with real goals and constraints, is something else entirely.

2

Why This Matters - The ROI of an IEC

Families often ask me whether working with an IEC is "worth it." When viewed through a return-on-investment lens, the answer is increasingly clear:

Improved outcomes: According to the Independent Educational Consultants Association (IECA), students who work with an IEC are admitted to one of their top-choice schools at a significantly higher rate than the national average.

Financial efficiency: Strategic college list building can reduce over-applying, avoid costly misaligned schools, and increase eligibility for merit aid. Even a modest merit scholarship can offset or exceed the full cost of consulting services.

Time savings: Parents spend hundreds of hours researching colleges, deadlines, and requirements. An IEC consolidates this effort into a guided process, saving time and reducing friction within the family.

Avoiding costly mistakes: Missed deadlines, misinterpreted requirements, poorly positioned applications, or ill-fitting school choices can cost families thousands of dollars in lost opportunities or transfer expenses later.

Navigating a Rapidly Changing Landscape

Academic trends are not static. Colleges regularly adjust:

Test policies (test required, test-optional, test-blind)
Available majors and program capacity
Class sizes and enrollment goals
Essay prompts and interview expectations
Extracurricular emphasis and institutional priorities

Relying on outdated assumptions, or anecdotal advice, can put students at a disadvantage. My role is to stay current with these shifts and help families make informed decisions rooted in real data, not guesswork.

The Bigger Picture: Fit, Focus, and Confidence

Timelines matter and communication is essential; I cannot stress this enough. When expectations are clear and the process is structured, families experience fewer arguments, less confusion, and a more focused applicant. Most importantly, students gain ownership of their journey.

It is time for your child to move into the driver's seat. With your support and my professional guidance, your child's college list will be intentional, balanced, and realistic, containing multiple colleges that truly match their academic profile, interests, and long-term goals. The result is not just better admissions outcomes, but a smoother process and a stronger start to college life.

Even with the best data and guidance, there comes a point when strategy alone is no longer enough.

This is the moment when parents must shift roles, from planners to supporters and allow their child to fully step into ownership of the journey ahead.

3

From Driver's Seat to Passenger Seat

When my own daughters began their college search process, I was, admittedly, thrilled. As both a parent and, at the time, a pro bono essay editor, I couldn't wait to take the journey with them. I looked forward to reliving my own meaningful college years through their eyes, revisiting campuses, conversations, and possibilities that once shaped me.

But as the process unfolded, I began to notice something uncomfortable: my own biases were quietly creeping into their experience.

As parents, we spend years shaping our children's moral compass, values, and sense of responsibility. And then, almost suddenly, we are asked to step back. To trust. To let go. I will be the first to admit that this transition is not easy. The college admissions process, perhaps more than any other milestone, tests a parent's ability to balance guidance with restraint.

At its best, this process is a rare opportunity for parents to truly *see* their children, to understand their hopes, fears, values, and ambitions, all expressed in their own voice. But when parental expectations begin to overlap with a student's path, confusion can set in quickly for everyone involved.

This is the moment for parents to pause and remember a few important lessons:

> **Honor your family's ethical standards—without inserting your voice.**
> The values you have instilled over the years are already part of your child; they do not need to be rewritten into their essays. Resist the urge to "improve" their story by shaping it into something that

13

sounds more polished, impressive, or familiar to you. Be proud of their voice and protect it. This is, after all, their moment to shine.

Be honest about how college data aligns with your child's data.

Encouraging a student to overreach or, just as damaging, to underestimate themselves often leads to stress, disappointment, and frustration. Realistic expectations grounded in data help everyone move forward with clarity and confidence. When goals are honest and aligned, the finish line feels far more rewarding.

Model gratitude, service, and respect.

These values are deeply connected. Gratitude fosters humility, service builds perspective, and respect, both for oneself and others grows from both. Shared service experiences can be especially meaningful during this time. They create space for genuine connection, often opening doors to conversations you might not otherwise have. In those moments, your child may offer you a rare glimpse into their inner world.

For years, parenting has often meant telling our children what to do and what not to do. This phase asks something different of us. Now is the time to ask, **"What do you think?"** and to truly listen to the answer.

It is also the time to observe rather than direct. Watch your child during campus visits. Notice their reactions to the people, the environment, the energy of a place. See what excites them, what makes them hesitate, what lights them up. Look at them with pride, they have earned the opportunity to be here.

As parents, your most valuable role now is that of a supportive onlooker and trusted passenger. There will be bumps, potholes, moments of fear, and inevitable "uh-oh" realizations along the way. But you will get there. And the real success is not just reaching the destination; it's arriving there together.

Did You Know?

The strongest college applications are honest, aligned, and personal.

College admissions success isn't about chasing numbers or prestige. It's about understanding the data, adapting to a changing landscape, and knowing when to step back so students can take ownership of their journey.

When strategy and support are aligned, the process becomes clearer, calmer, and far more effective.

Part II: Building the Foundation

4

Starting Early - The Smartest Advantage in Your College Admissions

There is a clear, proven process I use with my students and their families, one that leads to stronger outcomes and a far less stressful college application experience. At the heart of this process is one simple principle: **starting early matters.**

I'm often asked, "What's the advantage of beginning the college process early?" The data is consistent and compelling. Students who start early are more successful in gaining acceptances, make better strategic decisions, and experience significantly less stress along the way.

To be clear, starting early does not mean applying early. It means that the moment you set foot in high school is the moment to begin thinking intentionally about what comes next, academically, personally, and strategically.

If you're considering college, it helps to understand the landscape. According to the latest data, (2023-24) there are roughly 6,000 colleges and universities in the United States, about 2,700 of which are four-year institutions. Of those, only around 20% of schools admit fewer than 50% of applicants. The remaining four-year colleges have an average acceptance rate of approximately 67%. Understanding where colleges and universities fall within this range is essential to building a realistic and balanced list.

One of the most significant trends in recent years is the growing impact of early application options, including Early Decision (ED I and ED II) and Early Action (EA). Colleges are now filling a much larger portion of their incoming classes during early rounds, often leaving fewer seats available during Regular Decision. As a result, many students are deferred rather than denied, which adds uncertainty and prolongs stress.

This is why I strongly encourage students to begin their Common Application early. Once you start, your work is saved as you go, allowing you to make steady progress over time. This approach reduces pressure, enables thoughtful reflection, and helps avoid the rushed, and often sloppy mistakes that come with last-minute deadlines.

A well-considered application strategy is the foundation of success. Building that strategy requires clarity around your college list during the spring and summer before senior year, careful consideration of admissions deadlines, and a realistic review of recent acceptance data. Together, we evaluate where you truly fit, ensuring your list includes the right balance of safety, target, and reach schools.

Let's be honest: completing college applications takes a significant amount of time. It is commonly reported that admissions officers typically spend only 8–15 minutes per application (sometimes even less) between initial read, second read, and (if needed) committee discussions. That's why I stress the importance of putting your best foot forward, highlighting the experiences, achievements, and qualities that most clearly demonstrate why you belong at a particular school.

Applying to college is a serious undertaking and should never be taken lightly. But it doesn't have to be overwhelming. With the right planning, perspective, and pacing, the process becomes manageable and even empowering.

In the chapters ahead I'll walk you through this process step by step, providing the insight, structure, and strategy you need to move forward with confidence and ultimately achieve your college admissions goals.

5

The GREAT Course Dilemma

Students often ask me which courses colleges and universities consider the most rigorous when evaluating an applicant. My answer is always the same: take courses that will give you a positive experience, while still challenging you appropriately.

AP (Advanced Placement) courses are designed to prepare high school students for college-level work and may provide college credit depending on exam scores and institutional policy.

DE (Dual Enrollment) courses are college classes taken during high school, at a local college, online, or sometimes taught at the high school by an approved instructor.

IB (International Baccalaureate) is a rigorous, internationally recognized curriculum designed to prepare students for higher education.

Let's break it down.

If students want to save money or potentially graduate early, they may load up on DE courses, sometimes earning an associate degree while still in high school. DE can appeal to many colleges because core courses (English, math, lab sciences, social sciences) often transfer as equivalents, saving time and money. *Remember:* not all DE courses transfer, most colleges and universities now offer equivalency charts to help guide you.

Most U.S. high school students take Advanced Placement (AP) courses, and for good reason. AP classes offer a more rigorous academic experience, allow students to learn alongside highly motivated peers, and provide a glimpse of what college-level work feels like. For many students, they are the first real stretch academically, and that stretch matters.

At more selective colleges and universities, AP coursework is no longer just "nice to have." These schools expect students to challenge themselves within the opportunities available at their high school. In fact, some elite institutions now openly state that they expect to see AP, IB, or similarly advanced coursework on a student's transcript whenever it is offered.

This does not mean students should overload themselves or take AP classes just to impress colleges. But it does mean that avoiding academic rigor can quietly limit options later. Admissions officers are not simply counting APs; they are looking for evidence that a student chose the most challenging path that was reasonable for them and followed through with effort and integrity.

In short, AP courses are not about perfection or pressure. They are about showing readiness for the level of thinking, writing, and problem-solving that college will require.

So, which should you choose? This is where I can help evaluate your interests, learning style, teacher input, transfer accuracy, academic maturity, and the offerings available at your high school.

Ultimately, colleges and universities focus on two core questions when they read your transcript. First, did you challenge yourself with the most rigorous courses available to you at your high school? Second, once you stepped into those classes, how well did you perform?

Admissions officers are not simply counting the number of advanced courses you took; they are evaluating your choices in context. They look at what your school offered, what path you chose within those options, and whether your grades show that you were able to handle the level of difficulty you selected. In the end, keeping a thoughtful, balanced, and straightforward course load tells them the most about your readiness for college-level work.

6

KEYS to College Acceptances

Course selection is one important piece of the admissions puzzle, but it is far from the only one. Colleges evaluate students as whole people, not just transcripts. That's where the next set of KEYS comes into play.

Answer the college's questions.

When schools ask why you want to attend, be specific. Do their programs align with your academic interests? Are you drawn to their location, campus culture, or study-abroad opportunities? Thoughtful, detailed answers show genuine interest and help colleges see how you would fit into their community.

Pay attention to what colleges value.

If a college asks about community service, leadership, or involvement, that's a signal. Those questions reveal what they care about. When students engage intentionally in activities that matter to them, and that align with what schools emphasize, it strengthens both their application and their sense of purpose. Colleges don't expect perfection, but they do look for consistency, contribution, and authentic engagement. Over time, students begin to see themselves not just as applicants, but as future members of a campus community.

Keep an open mind.

Set aside assumptions and truly listen to what each campus is telling you, especially when you visit. A school you once dismissed may be the one that surprises you the most. That's the power of approaching the process with curiosity instead of certainty.

Time is on your side.

Activities, clubs, and leadership roles matter, not only because they strengthen applications, but because they help students discover who they are and what they care about.

When my eldest daughter was searching for colleges, she had one clear favorite. But she stayed open to the process. She took the visits, asked the questions, and let herself experience each campus fully. On her way home from one visit, I received a text that said, *"Mom, this is where I'm going to college."* And it wasn't the school she originally had in mind.

These keys matter most when the timeline begins to accelerate, which, for most families, happens in junior year. Once the foundation is set, the process begins to move faster, and knowing what to expect, and when, becomes essential.

As you move forward, keep these keys in mind. This is YOUR journey, and you hold the KEYS to your college kingdom.

Did You Know?

Colleges evaluate your transcript in context of what was available at your high school. That means course choices made as early as 9th grade quietly shape your options years later, long before essays or test scores enter the picture.

Part III: The Timeline Matters

7

Junior Year - When the College Journey Becomes Real

Junior year is the moment the college journey shifts from abstract to unavoidable. Sometime during the second semester, a student who once felt comfortably distant from the process suddenly realizes: **this is no longer theoretical, it's real.**

Excitement builds. Nerves follow. Parents often feel the urgency even before students do.

This is when I begin working more closely with students as they transition from "high schooler" to "college applicant." The change isn't dramatic, but it's unmistakable. Focus sharpens. Deadlines carry weight. Effort becomes intentional as many of my students begin marking submission dates on their calendars, their road behind them starts to inform their road ahead.

This is the year when details begin to matter, and small choices compound. We start by revisiting your child's extracurricular activities, going beyond a simple list. Together, we examine commitment, leadership, growth, and impact to shape a resume that tells a clear and credible story.

College visits take on new importance as well. Campuses are no longer just interesting places to walk around; they become environments students actively evaluate. They begin paying closer attention to academics, culture, opportunities, and whether a school truly aligns with what they want next.

By the end of junior year, students are no longer passengers in the process. **They're taking the wheel.** The road ahead is coming into focus, and momentum is building toward what comes next.

8

Buckle Up! Senior Year Is No Joke

In fact, it may be the most emotionally chaotic chapter yet (at least so far). I often tell families it's like living with Sybil… remember the girl with multiple personalities? That's your senior: confident one moment, overwhelmed the next, thrilled, terrified, indifferent, motivated, all within the same afternoon.

The excitement starts bubbling up around early June, before senior year, when we open the Common Application together for the first time and the "real" work begins. Until now, your student has been guided by teachers, counselors, parents, grandparents, coaches, essentially anyone older and breathing (or at least that's how they see it).

They know this matters. Everything they've done, the grades, activities, choices, late-night study sessions, lead to this moment. They feel the weight, the pressure, and the itchy anticipation of what's coming next. They may not be packing quite yet, but the launch is real, and both of you can feel it.

Here's the hard truth: the Common App isn't just "a form." It's a lot; far more than what we ever dealt with. There are two major sections, dozens of subsections, hidden mini-questions, and little details that matter. Filling it out correctly can sometimes feel like summiting Kilimanjaro in flip-flops.

The good news is that a large portion of the Common App can and should be completed over the summer: the profile information, family background, activities list, honors, and testing history. Getting those pieces done early means that when school starts, your student isn't drowning in paperwork while also juggling classes, sports, rehearsals, volunteering, jobs, etc. Believe me, this is one of the "Most Common Mistakes."

Then comes the essay (trust me, students find this piece way more daunting than expected). This is why we begin the personal statement early and aim to have it written, revised, and finalized before fall even arrives. When that main essay is finished ahead of time, it removes a massive weight from senior year and makes every supplemental essay that follows feel far more manageable.

Once the personal statement is complete, the next layers are supplemental essays, short answers, and sometimes interviews, one for each school on their list. This is exactly why building a thoughtful college list matters so much. The list determines not only where your student applies, but how much writing they will need to do, which deadlines matter, and how much time and energy is required to stay organized and on track.

We also begin resumes in early spring of junior year, so by the time applications open, students are not scrambling to remember what they did over the last four years. Their accomplishments, leadership roles, work experiences, and service are already documented and ready to be shaped into applications, essays, and interview answers.

After a few months of steady effort, juggling applications alongside school, extracurriculars, jobs, friends, and life, it all comes together. They grow. They stretch. They learn resilience. And yes…they really do finish.

So, parents… breathe. Be patient. Offer snacks. Let them drive (even when it feels like they're taking the scenic route).

You can survive this year!

And I'm here so you don't have to go through it alone.

By the time senior year is underway, most families realize something important: this process is no longer theoretical. It is time-bound, emotionally charged, and filled with decisions that carry real consequences.

Up to this point, the focus has been on **when** things happen. With the timeline accelerating and emotions running high, the next step is learning **how** to interpret the signals colleges are sending, and **how** to respond strategically.

Did You Know?

Students who complete application groundwork over the summer often submit stronger, more thoughtful applications, not because they are better writers, but because they are less rushed.

Summer preparation also reduces avoidable mistakes. The Common Application includes far more detail than many families expect, and last-minute submissions have higher error rates, including misreported courses and activities.

Part IV: Reading the Signals

9

Using the Signals to Guide Your College List

When creating a thoughtful and confident college list, I prefer to move away from labels like safety and reach. Admissions decisions are not binary; they are contextual. I encourage students to focus on the signals their academic profile sends and how those signals align with fit.

I use a more directional guide with my students through a **red light, yellow light, green light** strategy, one that is rooted in data but centered on fit.

Let's walk through how this works together.

Students begin by identifying the criteria that matter most to them. Cost, location, size, academic offerings, campus culture, and learning environment all play an important role. Once these factors are clearly defined, we're layering in academic data, GPA trends, test score ranges, and admissions patterns to help shape a well-balanced list, leading you to pay attention to the signals.

Green light schools are where the data aligns strongly with your profile and your priorities. Your GPA and test scores are at or above the school's averages, and the institution checks the boxes that matter most to you. These are schools where the indicators suggest you are well positioned for admission *and* success. I typically recommend narrowing this category to **four to six schools**.

Yellow light schools require a bit more consideration. The data is still encouraging, but there may be elements that warrant caution. Perhaps the academic averages are slightly above your current profile, a program is evolving, or a factor like location or campus setting isn't an obvious match, but you can still envision yourself there. These schools deserve thoughtful evaluation and honest reflection. I recommend adding **two to three yellow light schools** providing a healthy balance.

Red light schools are those that may be more competitive academically or have requirements that extend beyond your current profile. However, they remain on the list for a reason. You can clearly picture yourself thriving on the campus, pursuing a specific major, or growing into the opportunity, whether through a deferral, waitlist, or even a future transfer path. These schools can be worth visiting and exploring, as long as they are approached with perspective. I generally recommend **one or two red light schools** at most.

At the end of the process, the goal is not simply to gain admission, but to land in a place where you can grow, succeed, and feel at home. You want to avoid an environment where you are constantly struggling just to keep up, just as much as one that fails to challenge or inspire you. This strategy is about clarity, balance, and intention, using the lights not to limit your options, but to guide you toward your best possible fit.

Once a list begins to take shape, the next step is understanding how colleges evaluate one of the most debated signals of all: standardized testing.

10

Test Optional, Test Blind, TEST Smart!

When working through applications, I find that students often stress most over their test scores. Standardized test scores were once considered a cornerstone of admissions. Today, they are one signal among many, and one that colleges now use with far more nuance. Understanding what test optional and test blind policies truly mean is essential to deciding when scores help, when they don't, and when they may unintentionally weaken an application.

As a result, more institutions have adjusted their testing policies. **Test-optional** means students may choose whether or not to submit standardized test scores as part of their application. **Test-blind** (sometimes called test-free) goes a step further. Scores are not considered at all, even if a student submits them. While some colleges have recently returned to requiring test scores, the broader trend toward flexibility remains significant. For that reason, I advise my students to consider including a mix of schools that are test-optional and that require test scores when building a balanced college list.

Commonly reported data ranges currently state that more than 2,000 four-year colleges and universities in the United States are test optional, with roughly 400 of those institutions making the policy permanent. That said, "test-optional" does not always mean "test irrelevant." Many schools still consider scores for merit-based scholarships, honors programs, or final admissions decisions when additional context is needed. Understanding how each college uses, or does not use, test scores is critical.

So how should students decide whether to submit their scores? My general rule is simple: **if your test scores align with your GPA or fall at or above the school's published averages, submitting them can strengthen**

your application. In that case, the scores reinforce your academic profile. If, however, your scores are noticeably below average or do not match the strength of your transcript, it is worth carefully evaluating whether they add value or create doubt.

Academic data shows that students today are taking increasingly rigorous coursework, including Advanced Placement (AP), International Baccalaureate (IB), and Dual Enrollment (DE) classes, sometimes beginning as early as middle school. At the same time, standardized tests like the SAT and ACT have continued to evolve, often emphasizing specific strategies and testing skills that do not always reflect classroom learning or long-term academic success.

I have seen this firsthand with many students, including my eldest daughter. She was a strong student with rigorous coursework and finished near the top of her graduating class, but standardized testing was a persistent challenge. Her college of choice required test scores at the time, and despite tutoring and repeated effort, she never truly mastered the ACT. The stress was significant. She eventually raised her score enough to earn an academic scholarship, but the test never reflected her true academic ability. Four years later, she graduated cum laude with a double major, rendering that test score largely irrelevant.

Admissions officers understand this reality. They review applications holistically and often expect a reasonable alignment between GPA and test scores. When that alignment does not exist, test-optional policies allow colleges to focus on the fuller academic picture, course rigor, grades over time, teacher recommendations, and overall fit. This approach gives students who struggle with standardized testing a more level playing field without lowering academic standards.

Ultimately, colleges and universities continuously evaluate which data best predicts student success. As admissions practices evolve, the goal remains the same: identifying students who will thrive academically and contribute meaningfully to the campus community. Understanding how test policies work and how to navigate them strategically empowers students to present themselves in the strongest possible way.

Once students understand whether test scores should be submitted, the more practical question follows, when to test, how often, and which exam best reflects their strengths.

11

ACT / SAT Timing, Attempts, and Strategy

Each year, when the ACT and SAT release their test dates, students begin asking me how many times they should take the exam. My answer is always the same: let's see how you do the first time and how you feel about the test before deciding what comes next.

There are **no formal rules** on how many times a student can sit for the ACT or SAT. I've worked with students who took the SAT four or more times before switching to the ACT and testing once and others who did the opposite. Some students take both exams and ultimately submit the one that best reflects their strengths. I've also had students test just once, while others sit six or more times.

The good news is that you only need to submit one score, and most colleges still superscore, meaning they take the highest section scores across multiple test dates and combine them for the best overall result. A small number of highly selective schools do not superscore and require a single test sitting, so it's important to know each college's policy.

Before deciding how many times to test, it's important to step back and consider a few practical factors. Start by researching the testing policies of the colleges on your list. Some schools superscore, meaning they combine your highest section scores across multiple test dates, which can make additional sittings work in your favor. Others look only at a single test score, in which case it may be smarter to prepare more thoroughly and limit testing to one to three attempts.

Your prior performance can also offer useful clues. A strong PSAT score often signals that the SAT may be a good fit, since the PSAT closely mirrors the SAT in both structure and content. On the other hand, students

43

who are particularly strong in science and math may feel more comfortable with the ACT, which includes a dedicated science section. While some colleges now treat that section as optional, schools evaluating students for STEM-related majors often pay close attention to those scores.

If you're unsure which test aligns best with your strengths, official practice exams are the most reliable way to decide. Practice tests from College Board and ACT provide the most accurate representation of question style, timing, and pacing, making them an essential starting point. Finally, consider your personal schedule. Students deeply involved in sports, performances, or activities with heavy weekend commitments should plan strategically around testing seasons. If fall is packed with games, rehearsals, and travel, spring test dates may be a better fit, or vice versa. Thoughtful planning can make the testing process far more manageable and far less stressful.

If possible, I generally recommend that students take at least one official test during sophomore year. This provides a baseline score and helps determine whether tutoring is needed, which test is the better fit, and the best time of year to test. Of course, many students do end up successfully taking the test later in high school so there's no need to stress about taking it early. Most importantly, we reassess together and make intentional decisions about future sittings.

Only after understanding all of these factors can you make an informed decision about how many times you should take the ACT or SAT.

12

Building a Strong GPA the Right Way

While testing is episodic, your GPA tells a longer story, one that unfolds over four years and carries significant weight in every admissions review.

Colleges are not simply evaluating grades; they are evaluating choices, rigor, and growth over time. Understanding how GPA is read helps families avoid short-term strategies that undermine long-term success.

GPA: grade point average is a numerical snapshot of a student's academic performance, typically calculated on a 4.0 scale. While the number itself matters, colleges never view GPA in isolation. They evaluate it in context: the courses taken, the rigor of the curriculum, and how a student challenged themselves relative to what their high school offers.

This is where confusion often arises.

Some families believe that taking only on-level courses will automatically lead to a "better" GPA and therefore a stronger application. During an early client meeting, a parent mentioned that one of his colleague's children was taking "easy" courses to boost their GPA. I clarified, that while this approach may produce a higher number, it often fails to demonstrate what colleges value most: **academic curiosity, appropriate challenge, and readiness for college-level work**.

Course Rigor Matters. But So Does Fit.

High schools offer multiple course levels for a reason. They are designed to meet students where they are academically while still encouraging them to grow. Building a strong GPA is not about taking the hardest possible schedule or the easiest path to straight A's. It comes from choosing classes that fit your natural strengths and genuine interests, introduce the right amount of challenge, and create space to succeed while still being pushed to improve.

When the balance is right, students are both confident and stretched. They stay engaged, develop deeper skills, and earn grades that accurately reflect their ability. That combination of thoughtful course selection and solid performance is what creates a transcript that stands out for the right reasons.

If you are earning strong grades in honors or advanced placement courses often it sends a more compelling signal than earning slightly higher grades in exclusively on-level classes, especially at selective colleges. Admissions officers understand that an "A" in an advanced placement course often reflects greater rigor than an "A" in a standard one.

Depth Over Short-Term Gains

Colleges also look for patterns:

Are students progressing to more challenging coursework over time?

Are they pursuing depth in areas of interest such as math, science, humanities, or the arts?

Are they willing to challenge themselves, even when perfection isn't guaranteed?

A strong GPA reflects **sustained effort, resilience, and intellectual engagement**, not avoidance of challenge.

The Right Strategy

The most successful students are not the ones chasing the highest possible number on a transcript. Instead, they are the students who choose rigorous courses where it makes sense, perform well within that level of challenge, and build an academic record that clearly tells a story. Over time, their transcript reflects growth, thoughtful exploration, and genuine readiness for college-level work.

In short, it is always in a student's best interest to take the courses that are **right for them**. A confident, well-built GPA balances challenge and performance, and when viewed in context, it becomes far more meaningful than the number alone.

Of course, even the best-intentioned academic paths can encounter a misstep. Academic and emotional setbacks, such as, withdrawing from a challenging course or encountering a personal conflict are common. What matters most is how students respond, as those decisions can be as telling as grades or scores.

13

Growth Over Perfection

Perfection has never been the standard for college admissions. **Growth is.** Colleges expect students to make mistakes; what matters is honesty, accountability, and reflection. When addressed thoughtfully, setbacks often strengthen an application rather than weaken it.

I can tell you this with confidence; I am far from perfect, and I know many of you reading this can say the same. Most students experience a few missteps during their high school years. Mistakes, failures, and poor decisions are part of growing up. The good news is that the Common Application now addresses this reality directly, and as an Independent Educational Consultant (IEC), that is reassuring rather than stressful.

Colleges and universities share a clear and universal expectation: incidents must be disclosed during the application process. If a student fails to report an issue and the truth is uncovered later, institutions reserve the right to rescind an offer of admission or even expel a student. **Transparency matters.**

The Common App includes specific sections designed to address a wide range of incidents. My advice is always the same: disclose the situation and explain it honestly. Some colleges may request additional details or documentation, such as school records, but this process gives students the opportunity to explain what happened in their own words and, more importantly, how they learned and grew from the experience.

In short, making a mistake does not define you. Colleges are not averse to mishaps; in fact, many view them as powerful moments of growth and maturity. These experiences can become meaningful parts of an application when handled thoughtfully and responsibly.

I saw this firsthand while attending an accepted student day with my youngest daughter at one of her top-choice schools. During a student-led discussion, a young man openly shared how he struggled academically during his senior year of high school. He explained the circumstances, took responsibility, and described how he addressed the issue directly in his college applications. In the end, he received just one denial and wasn't even sure it was related to that setback.

The bottom line is simple: high school is a four-year period filled with learning, growth, and change. Mistakes are part of life. When students are honest, reflective, and willing to show growth, most colleges and universities recognize and often reward that maturity.

Did You Know?

Colleges aren't just deciding who to admit, they're predicting who will thrive, persist, and graduate.

Admissions officers look beyond prestige, rankings, and isolated achievements. Course rigor, academic trends, engagement over time, and authentic interest all matter and help build "who you are" in their eyes.

A strong, holistic, application tells this story: this student is prepared, motivated, and likely to succeed here. When signals align with fit, colleges gain confidence, not just in admitting a student, but in seeing them graduate and grow.

Part V: Constructing Your List

14

Building a College List That Actually Works

If senior year feels like chaos, your college list is the control panel. The right list doesn't just improve outcomes; it reduces the workload and stress of everything that follows.

How to Narrow Options with Confidence, Clarity, and Purpose

When I begin working with students, their college list is either very long or surprisingly short and they frequently ask for my opinion on which schools to delete or add.

Let me explain. I worked with a student who, after several weeks, had narrowed his list to 32 schools. After a few meetings and several weeks of hard work on his Common App, he reconsidered and ultimately landed on his "sweet 16."

My perspective is this: while there are many factors to consider, successful college lists tend to follow a few timeless principles.

Here are FIVE standout takeaways I use to guide the process:

1. Focus on strengths. Keep test scores, coursework, and grades in perspective. Lean into your child's natural strengths, whether math, science, or the humanities, and target schools that will build on those talents.
2. Consider time commitments. If your child is deeply involved in outside activities, think about whether they want to continue or explore new ones in college. Look for schools that align with their preferences.

3. Match interests to opportunities. With many students taking AP or dual-enrollment courses, they often have a sense of their academic passions early. Choose schools that offer depth in those areas.

4. Consider cost. There's a saying: "It's not where you go, but what you do there that counts." This holds true in most cases. Unless you're pursuing a highly specialized degree available at only one institution, many schools offer similar majors and capable career centers. Keep tuition, living expenses, and debt load in perspective.

5. Be ready for change. Admissions trends shift, and a student's priorities may too. Keep the list diverse and adaptable throughout the process.

When your child is forming their college list, the return on investment (ROI) of these decisions matters. A strong, well-thought-out list can save time, money, and stress, and open more doors.

When you and your child look back, you want them to be able to say, intentionally:

"I would have been happy at any school on my list."

15

Financial Awareness - Understanding What College Really Costs

Moving through the college application process the cost of college is always a hot topic. College decisions are not only academic and emotional; they are also financial. Yet I see and work with many families entering the process focused on rankings, acceptance rates, and campus life without fully understanding what college will actually cost them.

That gap between expectation and reality is where stress often begins.

This chapter is here to help close that gap.

Let's make it simple, think of it like shopping for a car. The first number you see when researching colleges is the **sticker price**: tuition, housing, meals, and fees. At many private or out of state colleges, this can exceed $50,000 per year.

But, like purchasing the car, almost no one pays the full or sticker price.

For college, the number that truly matters is the net price; the real cost after scholarships, grants, and financial aid are factored in. For example, two families can send their children to the very same university and end up paying dramatically different amounts. What each family ultimately owes depends on a combination of their income and assets, the availability of merit scholarships, how financial aid formulas evaluate their circumstances, whether the student qualifies for in state or out-of-state tuition, and how generous that particular institution chooses to be with its own aid dollars.

In other words, the sticker price is only the starting point; the personalized net price is what determines whether a school is actually affordable.

This is why every family should use each college's **Net Price Calculator** before assuming a school is affordable or unaffordable. That tool provides the best estimate of what you are likely to pay.

There are two primary ways colleges help families pay for college:

Merit-based aid is awarded for:
> Academic achievement
> Leadership
> Talent (arts, athletics, etc.)

This money is often used to attract strong students and does not depend on family income.

Need-based aid is awarded based on:
> Income
> Assets
> Household size
> Number of children in college

This aid is determined by financial aid formulas and is designed to make college more affordable for families who qualify.

Some schools offer a great deal of both. Others offer very little merit aid and rely heavily on need-based assistance. Knowing which type of aid a school emphasizes is critical.

Why Early Decision Can Affect Financial Aid

Early Decision (ED) is a binding commitment. When a student applies ED and is accepted, they agree to attend that school.

This can affect financial aid in an important way.

Because the student is no longer comparing offers, the school has less incentive to increase scholarships or negotiate aid. While families can still appeal financial aid packages, the leverage they have is often reduced.

This does not mean ED is a bad choice. It simply means families should understand the financial implications before committing.

Why a "Dream School" Might Not Be Affordable

Unfortunately, one of the hardest moments in the college process is realizing that a favorite school is financially out of reach.

This happens more often than families expect.

Some schools offer generous aid. Others do not. Some give large merit scholarships. Others reserve most of their funding for need-based aid. A school's reputation does not guarantee affordability.

This is why building a college list must include **financial fit**, not just academic and emotional fit.

A dream school that creates financial strain can turn four years of excitement into decades of stress.

The right school is one that supports your goals and your future.

College is an investment. A powerful one. But it must be a thoughtful one.

Understanding the difference between sticker price and net price, knowing how aid works, and evaluating affordability early allows families to make confident, informed decisions, not rushed or regretful ones.

When finances are part of the plan, the college experience begins with clarity instead of fear.

16

Does Distance Matter? Finding the Right College Location for You

Once a strong list begins to take shape, another question inevitably follows: Where do I actually want to live for the next four years? Academic fit matters, but geography quietly influences everything from daily happiness to long-term growth.

When cultivating a college list, I often lead in with a simple question for my students: "Do you want to stay close to home for college?"

The answer I usually get is some version of: "It doesn't matter."

But does it?

While college is a time of growing independence and responsibility, let's be honest, being able to go home occasionally can be comforting. That raises an important follow-up question: how far away do you actually want to be? A short drive? A long drive? A flight?

When considering college location, here are several factors that students should thoughtfully weigh:

Weather preferences. Do you prefer warm or cold weather and not just occasionally, but most of the year? College lasts roughly nine months, spanning fall, winter, and spring. Summer weather often becomes irrelevant. When you imagine walking to an 8:00 a.m. class or heading back from a 6:30 p.m. lab, do you see yourself navigating snow and darkness, or lighter days and milder temperatures? That daily reality matters over four or more years.

School size and environment. Location often limits, or expands, your options. I once worked with a student who wanted a small school (under 10,000 students), with a liberal arts feel, within two hours of home. Unfortunately, given where she lived, that combination resulted in very few choices. We added several out-of-state schools, and she ultimately chose one about three hours away. Two years later, she hadn't even noticed the extra hour of driving home and she couldn't be happier.

Driving vs. flying distance. For many families, "driving distance" usually means about five to six hours. And often, that difference becomes irrelevant when other factors, academic fit, campus culture, or overall happiness, carry more weight.

Ultimately, deciding how close or far from home to attend college isn't about distance alone. It's about identifying what matters most to you and recognizing which factors are non-negotiable versus those that can be slightly compromised. Taking the time to reflect on these priorities will help you land in an environment that truly feels like home.

Once you've identified your preferred environment on a map, the next step is to test it in real life by stepping on campus.

17

Trying Colleges On - How Visits Reveal the Right Fit

Many of the details discussed so far begin to crystallize when students step onto campus. Visiting colleges turns abstract ideas, fit, culture, opportunity, into something tangible.

I often tell my students, **"You'll know where you want to go."** There's a reason this advice has become such a cliché.

Deciding where to go to college is a lot like deciding what to wear to school. Until you try something on, you don't really know how it's going to feel or fit. Colleges are the same way. Until you set foot on a campus, you can't truly know how it will feel to *you*.

I once worked with a student who was convinced she wanted a small liberal arts college in the Northeast. We built her list carefully around those criteria. As she visited campuses, she came back each time saying she could "see herself there," but her reaction was always lukewarm. No excitement. No spark.

During one of our meetings, I suggested she visit a larger school closer to home in the South. She was reluctant, but I wanted her to experience something different, something that might reignite her college excitement.

She went. That same afternoon, I received a text I still keep: **"I am applying here. I love it!"**

I worked with another student who was determined to return to his hometown for college. Although he lived on the East Coast, his heart was set on the West Coast. We explored those options extensively but eventually added a few East Coast schools as well.

He started by visiting nearby campuses. His interest grew. He visited more. Somewhere in the middle of that journey, he returned to his "hometown" school. It was exactly as he remembered, but suddenly, the distance felt overwhelming.

I've seen versions of these stories play out again and again. Students often fixate on location, size, or reputation based on what they've heard from friends, family, traditions, or even lifelong allegiance to a sports team. But those are just myths. Nothing compares to the reality of standing on a campus yourself.

And that experience matters in more ways than most families realize.

Just as important as how a campus feels to you is the fact that colleges care about seeing you on their campus as well. Visiting isn't only about discovery; it's also a signal of genuine interest. When you're interested in a person or a place, you show up and that presence matters. Colleges feel the same way.

That's why schools track campus visits. They note who attends, when they come, and how engaged they are. Some institutions even invite students to write a supplemental essay reflecting on their visit. Being physically present helps colleges imagine you as part of their community, just as much as it helps you imagine yourself there.

When both sides can picture the fit, that's when the process truly clicks.

But simply walking a campus isn't enough.

How you visit and what you do once you're there can make all the difference.

That's where the next chapter begins.

18

Beyond the Tour - Making College Visits Truly Count

As an Independent Educational Consultant, I visit college campuses throughout the year, whether for scheduled admissions tours, self-guided visits, or simply passing through a campus I haven't yet seen. Each visit offers valuable insight into a school's culture, layout, and academic environment.

However, when I began visiting colleges with my daughters, my perspective shifted. I was not only evaluating a campus professionally; I was searching for a place they could truly call home for four or more years.

During one of my youngest daughter's school breaks, we scheduled several out-of-state college visits. When we arrived at our first planned tour, we learned it had been abruptly canceled due to weather and staffing issues. Initially discouraged, we decided to make the most of it and explore on our own.

What followed became one of our most impactful college visits.

We spoke with faculty. My daughter sat in on a lecture. We ate in the dining hall, where we struck up conversations with current students who invited us to see their dorm room and shared honest insight about campus life. By the end of the day, she didn't just know about the school, she understood what it felt like to live there.

That experience reinforced an important truth: college visits aren't about checking a box. They're about paying attention.

The more you engage with a campus, the more clearly the right fit begins to emerge.

College Visit Do's and Don'ts:

Do take the official tour when possible. Student guides offer valuable perspective, and the questions others ask often spark insights you hadn't considered. You don't know what you don't know. And there truly are no "dumb" questions on a tour.

Do consider the campus in all types of weather. Your visit represents just one of the 140–160 instructional days you'll spend there, plus evenings, weekends, and winters. Imagine the campus in heat, cold, rain, wind, or snow.

Do eat in the dining hall and explore nearby food options. You'll be eating on or around campus most days. A strong dining program, or lack thereof, makes a real difference in quality of life.

Do talk with a professor or sit in on a class if possible. College is, first and foremost, about learning. Sitting in a lecture or speaking with faculty can offer invaluable insight. On one visit, a professor even shared an additional scholarship opportunity, proof that faculty can be an excellent resource.

Do see real housing options. If possible, tour an actual dorm room or learn about off-campus housing. If you know a current student, don't hesitate to ask to visit.

Don't discuss your admissions status during the tour. A visit is about gathering information, observing, and imagining yourself on campus, not about outcomes. Focus on exploring, taking notes, and experiencing what the school offers.

In the end, walking on the right campus should feel like putting on a brand-new shirt you can't wait to show off. You look around and see yourself rushing to class, meeting friends, attending events, and building your future.

The cliché works.

When it fits, you know!

19

Early Action, Early Decision, Regular Decision???

Once students understand where they want to apply, the next question becomes how and when to apply and that's where **Early Action, Early Decision, and Regular Decision** come in. This is where timelines matter and where strategy can significantly influence outcomes.

Fall is the busiest time of year for high school seniors, filled with college applications and big choices. After fun-filled campus visits, you start picturing football games, late-night study sessions, and coffee shop runs. Then comes the heart-thumping question: When should I apply to improve my chances?

Some colleges offer ED (Early Decision), some offer EA (Early Action), and all have RD (Regular Decision or Rolling Decision) deadlines. Each choice comes with specific dates and a list of required documents. As an applicant, it is in your best interest to decide which option is best for you.

There is a method to the madness.

Let's start with EA and ED. You're the student who has taken the ACT/SAT three or more times, worked hard on your GPA and extracurriculars, visited schools early, and narrowed your list with confidence. You can visualize yourself on these campuses. You're ready to commit to a timeline.

If you have no doubt that one college is the right fit, you may want to apply Early Decision. ED is a binding agreement: if accepted, you are committed to attend.

If you're not certain which school is your first choice, but your application is ready, Early Action may be the better move. EA is non-binding and often provides earlier results.

So, when does Regular Decision make sense? If you plan to take additional SAT/ACT tests, want to submit first-semester grades, need more time on essays, or want additional visits, those are valid and often wise reasons to apply RD.

Choosing your timeframe wisely matters. Each option brings excitement, commitment, and a bit of stress. Once your timeline is set, the next priority is protecting your plan from the common mistakes that can quietly undo months of work.

Did You Know?

Many colleges are not only deciding who to admit, they are also trying to predict who is likely to enroll.

Especially at mid-selective institutions, admissions offices manage enrollment carefully. Signals such as campus visits, information sessions, and consistent engagement help colleges assess whether an admitted student is likely to accept an offer.

Demonstrated interest isn't about checking boxes or chasing attention. It's about clarity. When a student engages intentionally, it sends a quiet signal of seriousness and fit, one that can matter when colleges are shaping a class and balancing their offers.

Part VI: Strengthening the Application

20

Common Mistakes (and How to Avoid Them)

Before, during, and after every application cycle, I am asked the same question in different forms:

What went wrong?

These mistakes don't happen because families don't care. They happen when good plans meet pressure, deadlines, and uncertainty.

The truth is that most families do many things right. They plan, they tour, they write, and they try their best to follow a thoughtful process. But even with good intentions, a few predictable mistakes can quietly derail an otherwise strong application journey.

You've already learned how to approach this process step by step. So, what can go wrong?

Here are the most common missteps, and **how to avoid them.**

Applying to Too Many Reach Schools: One of the biggest mistakes students make is building a list filled with schools that are far more selective than their academic profile supports.

Hope is not a strategy.

Your list should be grounded in real data: GPA ranges, test score averages, and recent acceptance trends. Trusting the numbers doesn't limit your dreams, it protects your options. A list that is too top-heavy leads to unnecessary disappointment and fewer choices in the end.

Waiting Too Long to Visit: As discussed in Chapters 17 and 18, visiting campuses is not just about you, it matters to colleges too. Schools track who visits, who engages, and who shows genuine interest.

High schools give students excused days for college visits for a reason. Use them.

Walking on campus, speaking with students, and sitting in classes provide insight you cannot get online, and they strengthen your application at the same time.

Writing Generic Essays: Colleges don't want perfect writing. They want honest writing.

Your essays are your chance to control the narrative and show admissions officers who you really are. Generic essays filled with vague statements and recycled phrases tell them very little. Specific stories, real experiences, and your authentic voice tell them everything.

This is how you turn an application into a connection.

Letting Parents Take Over: For years, students have had someone else in the driver's seat: teachers, coaches, counselors, and parents.

Now it's time for them to drive. (*in case you haven't noticed, I stress this a lot!*)

Parents play an essential role in supporting, encouraging, and guiding, but when they take control, students lose ownership of their story. Let your child steer. You'll be amazed how much they grow when they do.

And yes, it's okay to enjoy the ride instead of gripping the wheel.

Ignoring Fit: Fit matters more than prestige.

When choosing colleges, students sometimes chase names instead of environments. But you don't want to be a square peg trying to fit into a round hole. Use data. Listen to what current students say. Pay attention to how a campus feels.

The right school is the one where you will thrive, not the one that simply looks impressive.

The Bottom Line: Mistakes are inevitable. No one navigates this process perfectly. Trust your instincts!

But when you stay grounded in data, stay true to yourself, and make intentional choices, you avoid the biggest landmines. And that leads to what matters most: real options, real confidence, and a college experience that truly fits you.

21

Activities and Leadership Roles, RULE!

As students begin to picture themselves on campus, one question becomes increasingly important: **How will I show up there?** What students choose to do with their time both in high school and in college matters more than many realize.

One of the most powerful ways students create that fit and show colleges who they are is through how they choose to spend their time.

When you begin your college search, you'll hear it repeatedly on tours, in information sessions, and from admissions officers themselves: **it's important to be involved both in and out of the classroom.** Colleges and universities want strong GPAs and test scores, but they are also building a class of students with diverse interests, experiences, and perspectives. That's where extracurriculars come in.

Admissions officers are evaluating more than what you achieved academically. They're trying to understand who you are, what you value, and how you spend your time when no one is assigning you a grade. Your activities and leadership roles offer concrete evidence of your interests and a window into the kind of community member you may become on their campus.

As Brian Johnson, aka Anthony Michael Hall, says at the end of one of my favorite movies, *The Breakfast Club*: "You see us as you want to see us… But what we found out is that each one of us is a brain, and an athlete, and a basket case, a princess, and a criminal." That quote resonates because admissions officers are doing something similar: they're looking at what you present, how you answer questions, what you include (or leave out), and what your recommenders say about you, to build a full picture.

Here's the key: **Quality, not Quantity.**

Before you jump into everything, take a minute to think about where your interests naturally lie. When you enter high school, explore, volunteer, try clubs, play a sport, join organizations, or even create something new that you and others care about. As you become an upperclassman, narrow your focus. Go deeper. Take initiative. Aim to become a leader.

You have four years to establish involvement and grow into it. Your activities are more than "resume builders." They teach you how to work with others, serve your community, and discover what motivates you. When students approach involvement with intention, extracurriculars become a training ground for adulthood.

And yes, these experiences also help you stand out. But the real question is not, "How many things did you do?"

It's: **What do your choices reveal about who you are becoming?**

22

Why the Resume Is One of the Most Powerful and Overlooked Tools

When families think about college applications, they often focus on grades, test scores, and essays. Yes, all those matter. But one of the most underestimated tools, and one that can quietly open doors, is the **student resume.**

I often talk with students about the "keys to success" that unlock opportunities. Yet the key most often overlooked is a simple one: the résumé.

A resume is an account of accomplishments. I like to tell students it's their bragathon, a place to confidently and thoughtfully showcase what they've done throughout high school. And yes, I mean everything.

We begin working on resumes during junior year. And we continue to cultivate them until application time (occasionally later, if deferrals are involved). We work together, taking time, carefully articulating academics and extracurriculars to present the "holistic applicant" that colleges are seeking.

We begin with the basics: GPA, academic recognitions, and honor societies. From there, we move into extracurricular involvement. This is where the real work begins. Students often list participation, but colleges want more than attendance, they want impact.

Did you earn awards? How often? Over what period of time?
Did you lead, organize, create, mentor, or expand something?
Did you take initiative or deepen involvement year over year?

Colleges are looking for growth, responsibility, and engagement. They want to see how students used their time, and what they learned from it.

But a strong resume is more than a list. It tells a story.

It helps shape a student's identity, clarifies interests, and often reveals patterns that point toward a future major or career direction. In many ways, the resume becomes a mirror: a chance for students to understand themselves more clearly.

This is where depth matters more than volume.

If you played a sport for years, how did you grow, varsity level, leadership, mentoring younger teammates?

If you've played an instrument, did you join band, form a group, teach others, or perform in the community?

If you love animals, did you volunteer consistently, take on responsibility, or advocate for a cause you care about?

Purpose and progression are what transform activities into meaningful experiences.

A well-crafted resume is also one of the most valuable tools for essays and interviews. It's a built-in idea generator, a personal cheat sheet. And yes, college applications are a test… but this is one where you're allowed to bring notes.

A strong resume shows what you've done. Essays explain who you are. Together, they turn accomplishments into a story, and that story begins on the page.

23

Writing the College Essay - A Survival Guide (Yes... You Will Live)

Every summer before senior year, as essay season approaches, I watch a familiar phenomenon unfold, one I lovingly call **Senior Stall.**

Despite knowing for years that a college essay is coming, every rising senior somehow reaches the exact same moment: full stop, blank screen, existential crisis.

I've read hundreds of essays, and trust me: that wide-eyed look people usually reserve for deer in headlights? Students get the same expression the moment someone says, "Write about yourself."

First things first: **You are not alone.**

Writing is a process, not a personality test. For some, it takes days. For others, weeks. A brave few? Months.

There's no "right" timeline. (Except deadlines. Colleges invented those. Sorry.)

The myth: "I have nothing to write about." Meanwhile, your resume is two pages long.

Or this classic: "What do colleges want to know about me?" Answer: They want to know you, because you're what they're investing in.

And perhaps my favorite: "I can tell you everything about my best friend but nothing about myself." Really? Because you posted 25 selfies this weekend, you do know yourself. You just haven't tried to put it into words yet.

The confusion, the stomach flips, the dull ache of "What am I even doing?", yes. Normal. Welcome to the club.

The truth nobody tells you: nothing new must happen for a great essay to exist. You're not waiting for a defining moment, a dramatic story, or a sudden burst of inspiration. You're learning how to notice what's already there, the patterns, choices, values, and moments that shaped how you think and who you're becoming.

So instead of asking, "What should I write about?" try this:

Think of your essay as a **Writing Workshop**, not a test.

A Simple, Proven Way to Start:

Begin with a **moment**, not a message.

> **Where are you?**
> Put the reader somewhere specific. A room. A field. A bus. A kitchen table. A practice, a rehearsal, a late night. Details matter.
> **What's happening?**
> Describe what's unfolding in real time. Not the summary. The action. What are you doing? What's at stake in that moment?
> **Who's there (and who matters)?**
> This doesn't mean listing names. It means identifying whose presence shaped the moment, or whose absence did.

Once you've grounded the reader, you move **inward.**

> **How did this moment affect you?**
> What did you feel, notice, struggle with, or realize in the moment, or shortly after?
> **Why does it matter now?**
> This is where reflection lives. What changed because of this experience? How did it influence your choices, values, perspective, or growth?

If you're stuck, write badly on purpose. Bullet points. Fragments. Run-on sentences. No one sees the first draft. You're not trying to impress. You're trying to uncover.

A helpful way to think about strong writing is that the first half shows and the second half tells. You begin by putting the reader inside a moment with real scenes, actions, and people they can picture clearly. Then you step back and explain why that moment mattered, what you took from it, and how it changed or shaped you.

In other words, you first let the story unfold, and only after the reader has experienced it with you do you draw out the meaning and growth that came from it.

This structure isn't limiting; it's freeing. It gives you a place to start and a path forward. And once the words are on the page, shaping them becomes possible.

When you work through these steps thoughtfully, you'll end up with something powerful: a personal essay that sounds like you, not what you think a college wants.

Every senior feels overwhelmed at first. That's not a weakness; it's a sign you care. With guidance, reflection, and a little bravery, you'll produce an essay that is uniquely, confidently, unapologetically you.

And yes! **You will survive it.** (I've seen it hundreds of times.)

24

More Than a Requirement: Using Supplemental Essays to Your Advantage

When a college or university requests, or even offers, the *option* to submit **supplemental essays**, take it as an open invitation. This is your opportunity to share more about who you are beyond grades, scores, and activities, and to keep the school genuinely interested in learning more about you.

While the personal essay introduces your story and voice, supplemental essays allow you to continue the conversation in a more focused and intentional way.

Colleges often emphasize holistic review: no single component stands alone. Admissions officers evaluate your application as a whole. But essays, especially supplementals, offer something no transcript or resume can: insight into your personality, motivations, values, and how you think. These short responses help colleges understand not just what you've done, but why you've done it, and how those experiences have shaped you.

Supplemental essays usually ask very specific questions and require concise answers. Many schools cap these at 300 words, and some prompts are limited to 100 words or fewer. That brevity is intentional. **Colleges want to see whether you can reflect deeply and communicate clearly without filler.**

At their core, supplemental essays are designed to highlight you. Whether a prompt asks you to elaborate on an activity, discuss a book that influenced you, describe a leadership experience, or explain why you want to attend that institution, each response gives the reader "insider" knowledge about who you are.

There is a university in my area that has used the same supplemental prompt for over a decade. Over the years, I've read countless responses, many of them remarkable. Almost without exception, students initially feel stumped until they realize the truth: the college is not looking for a clever or manufactured answer. They're asking for an honest one.

That honesty is what admissions offices value most. Colleges aren't interested in answers that sound impressive but could apply to anyone. They want authenticity rooted in your real experiences, reflections, and interests. A genuine response, one that reflects who you truly are, will always be more compelling than a polished but impersonal one.

In short, supplemental essays aren't "extra" work. **They are essential opportunities.** When approached thoughtfully and authentically, they help you stand out, deepen your application, and show admissions officers why you belong on their campus.

25

A Note on AI and Authenticity

As students spend more time writing and refining their applications, a new question often arises: how, and whether, artificial intelligence should play a role?

I remind my students, share your information, authored by you.

When I was in high school, computers were the newest introduction. Many feared they would weaken thinking skills. Decades later, we learned how to adapt, using computers as tools, and ways to enhance our thinking. The same holds true for AI.

Artificial intelligence can be helpful for grammar checks, sentence clarity, and organization. Used appropriately, it can support the writing process. However, AI should never replace your work, your experiences, or your voice.

I frequently say to my students, "AI does not volunteer in the community. It does not study late into the night, prepare for exams, lead a club, perform on the field, rehearse an instrument, or dedicate hours to something meaningful. It does not grow, struggle, or persevere. You do."

That distinction matters!

Admissions officers are not looking for perfection. They are looking for authenticity. They want to understand who you are, what you care about, and how your experiences have shaped your goals. And after all, no one wants to read a story that is sterile or perfect.

So, while AI may help place a comma or refine a sentence, it cannot tell your story. Only you can do that. Be proud of your work. Share it honestly on your resume, in your essays, and in your interviews. Your voice is your greatest asset.

Colleges want to know the real you, with all your perfections and fabulous flaws!

Did You Know?

Applications feel strongest when essays, activities, and recommendations reinforce the same themes.

Admissions officers are not looking for students who do everything. They are looking for consistency and growth. When a student's interests, commitments, and reflections align across different parts of the application, it builds credibility and trust.

Trying to showcase every achievement can dilute the message. Strategic focus, where multiple pieces of the application point to the same strengths and values, often communicates maturity and clarity more effectively than volume.

A clear story is easier to believe, and easier to remember.

Part VII: Decisions and Outcomes

26

The Ultimate Decision

After years of planning, touring, late-night conversations, and hard work, accompanied by months of waiting, reflecting, and recalibrating, the moment finally arrives. Decisions are released and with them, a new kind of pressure.

College is no longer a "someday" idea. It's real.

And now comes the decision.

For many students, this is the biggest choice they've made so far. And surprisingly, the challenge isn't always getting in, it's choosing where to go. Multiple acceptances can quickly shift excitement into overwhelm, leading to what I often see at this stage: **decision paralysis**.

Why does this happen?

Because the criteria that helped students build a balanced list now requires them to narrow down to one school. Location, cost, size, majors, campus culture, everything that mattered before is suddenly competing head-to-head.

When applying, acceptance can feel abstract: a hopeful outcome, but still distant. Once results arrive, reality sets in. Early on, I often ask students, "If you're accepted, what would be your first, second, and third choice?" Some answer easily. Others say, "I'll just be happy to get in somewhere."

But happiness isn't the goal. **Fit is.**

This is where **revisiting matters.**

Accepted Student Days are one of the most powerful and often overlooked parts of the decision process. These events give students and families a chance to see campus through a different lens, no longer as applicants trying to impress a school, but as invited guests being welcomed into a community that has already said yes.

During these visits, students can sit in sample classes within their intended major, talk directly with professors and current students, walk through the residence halls, and get a realistic feel for what everyday life would look like if they chose to enroll. Instead of imagining what it might be like to attend, they can briefly live it, which often brings a level of clarity that no brochure, website, or virtual tour can match.

I cannot stress this enough: **attend them!** Even if you think you already know where you want to go.

The perspective shift is profound. Students are no longer visitors hoping for approval; they are evaluating a place that already wants them. That clarity is invaluable.

I've lived this personally. My youngest daughter was deeply indecisive, so we attended three accepted student days in one week. It was exhausting, but transformative. By the end, her decision was clear. Years later, as a college graduate, she still says, "That was the best decision I ever made."

And that's the goal: not just choosing a college but choosing with confidence.

Trust the process. Revisit your priorities. Give yourself the space and exposure they need to see themselves thriving. The right choice has a way of becoming clear once you truly step into it.

27

Deferral Directives - Deferred, Now What? Turning a Pause into Progress

Over the years, I've had many students receive a deferral decision. And while I wish I could say every deferral turns into an acceptance, but the honest truth is that it doesn't always happen.

What is true, however, is this: there are clear patterns and important lessons that can significantly improve a student's chances of moving from deferred to admitted.

Lesson #1: First-semester, senior year, grades matter more than ever. This is the most important piece of the puzzle. Admissions officers are watching closely for consistency, growth, and effort. They know senior year can bring "senioritis," especially for students who feel stuck in limbo. Students who maintain momentum send a powerful signal: This is someone who will thrive here.

Lesson #2: Don't step back from extracurriculars, lean in. Now is not the time to coast. In fact, this can be the perfect moment to demonstrate leadership and initiative. Winter and spring athletes might organize a team service project or take on a captain-like role. Others may pursue a part-time job, tutor younger students, or volunteer during school breaks. These experiences don't just strengthen a resume; they often reveal purpose.

Lesson #3: Respond thoughtfully and follow instructions exactly. A deferral is an invitation, not a rejection. This is an opportunity to reaffirm interest and show continued growth. Following directions carefully, meeting deadlines, and submitting meaningful updates can make a real difference. This is the place to demonstrate maturity, professionalism, and genuine enthusiasm.

The bottom line: A deferral means you are still very much in the game. With sustained effort, intentional choices, and the right guidance, a deferral can absolutely become an acceptance. This season isn't about waiting. It's about proving you belong!

28

Inconvenient, Tragic, or Ultimately Your BEST Choice?

I recently heard a simple but powerful question: "Is it an inconvenience, or is it a tragedy?"

That question immediately brought to my mind a conversation I had with a student who didn't get into his top-choice school. He was devastated. To him, the outcome felt final, defining, almost catastrophic.

Over the years, I've had countless versions of this same conversation with students and parents. They express disappointment, replay every decision, and ask what went wrong, why this school said no. Yet after a year spent at their second-choice school, those same students (and parents) often say something remarkable:

"I can't imagine being anywhere else."

So, let's return to the original question: **Is it really a tragedy if you don't get into your "dream school"?**

Here's the reality: you don't know what you don't know. You haven't attended classes. You haven't lived with a roommate, navigated campus life, eaten in the dining hall, joined clubs, or built relationships there. And yet, without experiencing any of it, the rejection can feel tragic.

Perspective matters.

A reminder worth repeating: your college list was built intentionally. Every school on it was one you said you would be happy attending, otherwise, why apply? Each one made the list because it offered something that fit you academically, socially, culturally, or personally.

97

That doesn't mean the disappointment isn't real. It is. For many students, this is their first true rejection after years of achievement. It's painful to invest so much energy and feel unwanted by a school that looked perfect on paper.

But this moment can also be pivotal. It's an opportunity to learn how not to take rejection personally and to recognize an important truth: sometimes the schools you think you want most aren't the ones where you will thrive most.

So, what initially feels like a tragedy often turns out to be a **temporary inconvenience.** One that, with an open mind, leads to a better fit, stronger growth, and ultimately a happier experience.

In hindsight, many students realize the "no" they feared most quietly guided them toward what became their best choice all along.

29

Bob's Story: The Dream School Transfer

A former student recently reached out with exciting news: he had *finally* been accepted to his dream school.

Let's begin. I'll call this student Bob.

Bob started his journey with me two years ago while attending College A. From the beginning, he knew he wanted to transfer to College B, but he wasn't sure how to get there.

When we began working together, we took a close look at his academic record, coursework, and intended major (which evolved slightly along the way). We identified a few gaps and created a plan to address them. Bob joined student organizations, volunteered in his community, and leaned into activities that highlighted his strengths. In doing so, he not only strengthened his application, but he also grew as a person.

A year and a half later, Bob submitted his transfer application to College B. He was first deferred, then rejected.

During the deferral period, I encouraged him to keep updating the admissions office with meaningful progress: new grades, leadership roles, and expanded volunteer work. He did. And more importantly, he never stopped striving toward his refined goals. Even after rejection, Bob remained disciplined, resilient, and hopeful.

Did you miss my opening line?

He got in.

Did You Know?

Deferrals are often strategic, not negative.

Colleges use deferrals to manage enrollment and gather additional information, not to signal disinterest. When a student is deferred, it often means the application remains under serious consideration, but the institution needs more context before making a final decision.

In many cases, deferrals reflect timing, class balance, or enrollment goals rather than a student's qualifications. While the waiting can feel discouraging, a deferral keeps the door open and preserves opportunity.

It is a pause, not a verdict.

Part VIII: When the Path Isn't Straight

30

Progress Is Not Always Linear

It is important to remember that during the college application process for some students, the story continues exactly as planned. But, for others, it takes a turn, and that turn is not a failure.

When the story bends or pauses, uncertainty often rushes in. Questions surface quickly. **Are we behind? Did we miss something? Is this a mistake?**

The truth is far simpler, and far more reassuring.

Not every student is meant to move forward on the same timeline or path. Growth does not follow a single script, and readiness is not measured by speed. Some students benefit from stepping back before stepping forward, taking time to reflect, mature, explore, or recalibrate before committing to their next chapter.

These choices are not signs of failure. They are often signs of self-awareness.

In today's admissions landscape, colleges are increasingly open to, and even appreciative of, non-linear paths. Students who arrive with greater clarity, purpose, and life experience often transition more successfully, persist at higher rates, and engage more deeply once they are on campus. A thoughtful pause, when used well, can strengthen both readiness and resolve.

This section is designed to normalize and clarify those alternatives.

Whether a student takes a gap year, begins at a junior or community college, or follows a less traditional route toward a four-year degree, the goal remains the same: to arrive prepared, confident, and aligned with the environment they are entering. What matters is not how quickly they get there, but how well the path chosen supports who they are becoming.

The chapters that follow provide practical guidance for families navigating these options. They outline what colleges expect, how applications work, and how to position non-traditional choices as intentional and strategic. More importantly, they offer reassurance that progress does not disappear when the timeline shifts, it simply takes a different shape.

A straight line is not a requirement for success.
Purpose, readiness, and confidence are.

31

The Road Back: Returning to College After a Gap Year

Gap years are one of the most discussed, and often misunderstood topics among families navigating the college admissions process. While many students move directly from high school into college, others may benefit from stepping off that path, for a period of time.

A gap year can provide space for reflection, growth, and exploration. Students may use this time to determine whether college is the right next step, gain real-world work experience, travel, pursue personal interests, or explore alternative pathways. The reasons for taking a gap year are deeply personal and, in many cases, necessary.

The most common question students ask me during this time is a practical one: **If I choose to return to college, what does that process actually look like?**

Returning to college after a gap year, whether that time away was carefully planned, unexpectedly extended, or simply unstructured does not have to feel complicated or risky. In fact, when approached thoughtfully, it can become a powerful part of your story. The key is to start by clearly defining your point of re-entry. Some students will be applying as true first-year applicants because they never enrolled in college. Others may need to apply as transfer students if they completed any college coursework during their time away. Still others may be returning to a school that previously admitted them after a deferment or withdrawal. This initial distinction matters more than many families realize, because it drives application type, requirements, deadlines, and even how financial aid is handled.

Even after time away, colleges will look closely at academic readiness. Your high school transcript still matters, including grades, course rigor, and overall GPA. Any college classes taken during the gap year will also be reviewed, along with standardized test scores if you choose to submit them. A well-used gap year can actually strengthen an academic profile. New skills, improved discipline, and demonstrated initiative often translate into stronger college performance. When appropriate, targeted coursework at a community college or through reputable online programs can reinforce that readiness and show that you are returning sharper, not rusty.

While colleges do not penalize students for taking a gap year, they do expect to see purpose behind the time away. Meaningful experiences might include employment, internships, apprenticeships, volunteer service, independent projects, creative or entrepreneurial work, educational travel, or professional certifications. What matters most is not the label of the activity but the evidence of growth, responsibility, and direction. You can usually explain this in an essay or the additional information section of the application, and sometimes in an interview. Remember, your tone should clearly show how the year provided perspective and prepared you to engage more fully in college.

Because every institution handles gap-year applicants a bit differently, it is essential to verify each school's specific requirements rather than relying on assumptions. Confirm whether you should apply as a first-year or transfer student, review any gap-year-specific essay prompts, check what types of recommendation letters are acceptable, and pay careful attention to deadlines. Some schools are flexible, others are not, and guessing wrong can cost you an opportunity.

Your recommendations may also need a refresh. A former high school teacher or counselor is often perfectly appropriate, but a supervisor or mentor from the gap year can add a valuable dimension. The strongest letters speak to maturity, reliability, and readiness to return to structured academics, not just past classroom performance.

Filing the FAFSA, and sometimes the CSS Profile, is still required. Income earned during the gap year may need to be reported, and families should ask directly how merit scholarships are affected. At some colleges, merit awards are reserved only for first-year applicants, so understanding those rules ahead of time can shape where and how you apply.

Like first year applicants, when you are building your college list, balance is important. Schools that appreciate non-traditional paths and emphasize advising and student support often serve gap-year students particularly well. A thoughtful mix of likely, possible, and aspirational choices keeps options open while reducing unnecessary pressure.

Before classes begin, invest some time in preparing for the academic transition back, this is easily overlooked. Refresh core skills in writing and math, rebuild consistent study habits, and make full use of orientation and advising resources. Connecting early with other students who took gap years can ease the social transition and provide a sense of belonging from day one. Most colleges and universities offer ways to connect with returning students through apps, visits, and social media outlets. Making use of these will help make your academic and social adjustment easier.

There are a few pitfalls worth avoiding. A gap year should never be framed as something to apologize for. Deadlines should never be assumed flexible without confirmation. Applications should clearly show growth and direction, not drift. And perhaps most importantly, students must be certain they understand whether they are applying under first-year or transfer rules before submitting anything.

When handled intentionally, a gap year is not a detour; it is often an advantage. Colleges are looking for students who used their time away to gain clarity, perspective, and purpose. The goal is to demonstrate that the pause did not slow the journey, **it strengthened the return.**

32

When Are Junior or Community Colleges the Right Choice?

I just discussed a gap year but not every reset involves time away, some involve choosing a different place to begin. For many students, this is where junior or community colleges come into play.

Junior and community colleges are often misunderstood, yet they can be an excellent, and strategic option for a wide range of students. These two-year institutions provide affordable academic, vocational, and technical education, offering associate degrees (AA, AS, AAS) and certificates. For many students, they serve as a bridge to a four-year university; for others, they offer a direct and efficient path into the workforce.

As college costs are constantly rising, one of the strongest advantages of junior and community colleges is affordability. They are especially appealing if you're planning to transfer (many offering direct and guaranteed pathways into colleges and universities), those paying for college on their own, or individuals balancing full-time work with coursework. Flexible class schedules, accessible faculty office hours, convenient parking, and smaller campus environments make them easier to navigate and manage. In some cases, students even gain access to nearby four-year university facilities or shared resources, without paying the higher four-year university cost.

These institutions also play a critical role in vocational and technical education. Many technical careers require targeted, hands-on training rather than broad general-education requirements. Junior or community colleges are designed to provide streamlined pathways that focus on practical skills, allowing students to enter the workforce sooner with relevant credentials.

For students eager to begin working quickly, this route is often the most efficient and cost-effective choice.

Junior and community colleges can also serve as a valuable steppingstone for student-athletes. I've had a few students go this route. Many four-year programs recruit from JUCOs, valuing the added maturity and academic readiness these athletes bring. This path can give the opportunity to extend both academic and athletic careers while refining skills and strengthening transfer opportunities.

Quick Summary

Affordable: Lower tuition and fees make college accessible and flexible.

Flexible: Ideal for working students, transfers, and self-funded families.

Career-Focused: Direct, efficient pathways into technical and vocational fields.

Transfer-Friendly: Strong bridge (or even a guaranteed pathway) to four-year colleges and universities.

Athlete Pathway: A proven option for extending academic and athletic development.

Junior and community colleges are not a fallback, they are a purposeful choice that can align powerfully with a student's goals, timeline, and financial reality.

Did You Know?

First time employers rarely ask where you started college, only where and how you finished in your major. In the long run, career opportunities are shaped far more by skills, experience, and perseverance than by the prestige of a starting point. Many successful students begin at junior or community colleges, take gap years, transfer, or follow less traditional paths before earning their degree.

Epilogue

This book is a passion project written for my past, current, and future students. It's important to know that I've experienced my own share of rejections, failed tests, and doubters. Yet here I am, still working hard, still believing, and now publishing the first of what I hope will be several books that will guide you in your college search.

My hope is that within these pages, you've found tools and stories, clarity and calmness to build your own toolbox; one that keeps you moving forward, strengthens your resilience, and helps you reach your dream school… or your dream, period.

The Admissions Edge Resources: Start Building Your Toolbox

Essay Writing Tips

- Don't stress over writing the perfect essay or figuring out what a college wants to hear.
- Don't fixate on writing what you think colleges want to hear.
- There are no "good" or "bad" topics. There are, however, stronger and weaker essays based on execution.
- Consider your values and philosophies.
- Ask: "What would everyone else say if they were writing about my topic?" Then discard that and write your story.
- Don't think: What have I done? Instead, think: How have I grown?
- Think "me," not "we."
- Uncertainty is okay.
- Vulnerability is powerful.
- Just because you did something impressive doesn't mean it will automatically make a great essay topic.
- Don't hunt for big words.
- Most importantly, sound like you.

YOU'VE GOT THIS!

College/University Terminology

Let's face it: when it comes to keeping up with our kids and their terminology, it can feel like a long, winding road with plenty of bumps. Even students aren't always "in the know" when it comes to college lingo. So, consider this your College/University Cheat Sheet.

RD (Regular Decision): the deadline by which all application materials must be submitted.

EA (Early Action): a non-binding option that allows students to apply and receive a decision earlier than Regular Decision.

ED1 (Early Decision I): a binding agreement stating that if a student is admitted, they are obligated to attend.

ED2 (Early Decision II): a binding option like ED1, but with a later deadline for students who need more time.

Rolling Admissions: Applications are evaluated as they are received, and decisions are released on an ongoing basis.

Official Visit: A registered campus visit (often including a tour and information session) that the college can record as demonstrated interest.

Unofficial Visit: A self-guided visit that is typically not tracked by the college and may not include staff-led programming.

FAFSA: Free Application for Federal Student Aid; the form used to determine eligibility for federal financial aid.

CSS: College Scholarship Service. An application for non-federal financial aid from specific colleges and universities, often private ones with large endowments, to determine eligibility for their institutional grants, scholarships, and loans.

Liberal Arts College: An institution offering broad programs in arts, sciences, and humanities with an emphasis on critical thinking.

Merit-Based Aid: Financial aid awarded based on academic achievement or other strengths, not financial need.

Net Price: The actual cost a family pays after grants, scholarships, and other aid are applied.

Pell Grant: A federal need-based grant for students with significant financial need.

Test Optional: a college or university that gives the student the option to include SAT/ACT scores with the application.

Test Blind or Test Free: a college or university will not consider SAT or ACT scores at all for admissions, even if an applicant submits them, focusing instead on GPA, essays, extracurriculars, and recommendations for a holistic review.

SAT: Scholastic Aptitude Test. A globally recognized, standardized test by the College Board, used by most U.S. colleges for admissions to measure high school students' readiness, assessing reading, writing, and math skills.

ACT: American College Testing. A standardized, curriculum-based college entrance exam to measure high school students' readiness for college-level coursework. It covers English, Mathematics, Reading, and Science.

Superscore: combines your highest section scores (like Math and Reading/Writing) from multiple test dates (SAT/ACT) to create a single, higher composite score.

The College Admissions Roadmap

The college process feels overwhelming because most families don't know what to do when. This roadmap gives you a clear timeline so you can move forward with confidence instead of panic.

This is not about pressure. It's about pacing.

9th Grade — Exploration & Foundation

Focus: Habits, curiosity, and getting involved
Students should:

- Adjust to high school expectations
- Build strong study habits
- Sign up for activities, clubs, sports, volunteering
- Begin discovering interests

Parents should:

- Encourage exploration, not specialization
- Support good routines and balance
- Avoid early pressure discussions, "top colleges"

10th Grade — Pattern Building

Focus: Strengths, consistency, and direction
Students should:

- Continue Building GPA and Course Rigor
- Narrow Extracurriculars to what they enjoy most
- Take a First SAT/ACT if appropriate
- Start Noticing what Subjects Excite them
- Narrow in on Extracurricular School and Non-School Activities

Parents should:

- Help them reflect on what's working

- Keep expectations realistic
- Begin learning about college types and costs
- Casually visit a few local colleges or universities

11th Grade (Fall) — Strategy Begins

Focus: Testing, visits, quality, and list building
Students should:

- Take or retake SAT/ACT
- Research Colleges and Universities that align with your qualifications
- Schedule a few official Campus Tours
- Build a preliminary College and University List
- Seek out Leadership Roles and Honors
- Search for Summer Opportunities that Align with potential Colleges or Majors

Parents should:

- Travel with purpose
- Track deadlines and requirements
- Help organize testing and visits

11th Grade (Spring) — Decisions Take Shape

Focus: Fit and readiness
Students should:

- Attend Campus Tours and College Information Sessions
- Narrow College and University List
- Choose possible Early Action or Early Decision schools
- Begin thinking about Personal Statement
- Finalize Senior-year Courses
- Begin Resume
- Continue to seek out Leadership Roles and Honors

Parents should:

- Talk openly about college cost, distance, and fit
- Begin financial aid planning

Summer Before 12th Grade — Execution

Focus: Writing, organizing, setting realistic application deadlines
Students should:
- Write Personal Statement and begin Supplemental Essays
- Complete First Section of Common App
- Finalize College and University list
- Finish work on Resumes

Parents should:
- Provide structure and support
- Help manage deadlines
- Encourage steady progress

12th Grade (Fall–Winter) — Submitting & Waiting

Focus: Follow-through
Students should:
- Complete All Sections of the Common App, and/or Specific College and University Apps
- Submit Applications; pay close attention to EA and ED deadlines
- Complete Interviews
- Complete Portfolios
- Update Resumes with any new achievements

Parents should:
- Stay calm
- Trust the process
- Avoid second-guessing
- Complete the FAFSA or CSS profile
- Stay away from the "rumor mill"

12th Grade (Spring) — Decision Time

Focus: Choosing the best fit
Students should:
- Attend Accepted Student Days
- Compare offers and Financial Aid
- Make Final Choice

Parents should:
- Ask good questions
- Support, not pressure, the decision

A clear roadmap replaces anxiety with momentum. When families know what season they're in, they stop feeling behind.

Questions Worth Asking on Your College Visits

A college visit is more than a tour; it is a chance to step into a college student's daily life and imagine what the experience might look like. Beyond the glossy brochures and scripted presentations, the most valuable insights often come from asking thoughtful, practical questions of the people who live and learn on campus every day.

Campus Life & Daily Experience

- What is it actually like walking to class in the winter or in bad weather?
- How spread out is campus, and how much walking is required on a typical day?
- What do students do on weeknights and weekends?
- Is the campus quiet, lively, or somewhere in between?
- What about joining a sorority, fraternity or club? What is offered and when?

Food & Living

- What is the food really like?
- Where do students actually eat most often?
- Are the best dining options included in the meal plan?
- How flexible are meal plans for students with dietary needs or busy schedules?

Housing

- Which dorms are considered the best for first-year students, and why?
- What is housing like after freshman year?

- Where do most upperclassmen live: on campus or off campus?
- How easy is it to get housing you actually want?

Transportation & Getting Around

- How hard is it to get a parking spot?
- Do most students bring cars?
- How reliable is on-campus transportation or shuttle service?
- Is the surrounding area walkable, bike-friendly, or transit-friendly?

Academics & Faculty Access

- How easy is it to schedule office hours with professors?
- Are professors approachable and available outside of class?
- Do students feel supported academically when they need help?

Opportunities Beyond the Classroom

- Ask to speak with a student who has studied abroad and learn what the experience was really like.
- Inquire about co-ops or internships. Do companies and recruiters visit campus?
- Ask about available research opportunities, whether tied to your major or led by a professor. Are some paid? When and how do you apply?

The College List Checklist - How to Build a Balanced College List

A strong college list is the foundation of a successful admissions process. It determines how many applications you will write, which deadlines you will face, how much stress you will carry, and how many real options you will have in the end.

The goal is simple: **Every school on your list should be a place you would be happy attending.**

To make that happen, your list must be balanced, realistic, and intentional.

Step 1: Understand the Three Types of Schools (using my "signals")

Every college on your list should fall into one of three categories:

Green Light Schools
These schools are where admission is reasonably possible but not guaranteed.

These are schools where:
- Your GPA and test scores are close to the school's averages
- Your coursework and activities match what the school values
- You have a competitive, but not automatic, profile

These schools often become your best options.

Yellow Light Schools
These schools are one where admission is highly likely and the cost is affordable.

A true yellow light means:
- Your GPA and test scores are above the school's average

- Your academic profile fits well
- You can afford the school if admitted
- You would actually be happy going there

If you wouldn't attend the school, it is not a real place to proceed.

Red Light Schools

These schools are more selective or competitive than your academic profile suggests.

This could be because:
- The school has a low acceptance rate
- Your GPA or test scores are below their average
- The school is highly selective for your intended major

Red light schools are exciting, but they should never be your entire list.

Step 2: Use a Balanced List Formula

A healthy college list usually looks like this:
- 4–6 Green light schools
- 2–3 Yellow light schools
- 1–2 Red light schools

That gives you enough options without creating unnecessary stress or application overload.

More schools do not equal better results. Smarter schools do.

Step 3: Ask the Right Fit Questions

For every school you consider, ask:

- Can I see myself living here for four years?
- Does this school offer strong programs in what I'm interested in?

- Do students seem happy, engaged, and supported?
- Would I be proud to call this school my college?

If the answer is "no" to any of these, take it off the list, even if the school has a great reputation.

Step 4: Check the Financial Reality

A college is not a real option if it is not affordable.

Before finalizing your list:
- Use the school's Net Price Calculator
- Learn whether the school offers merit aid
- Understand the difference between sticker price and actual cost

Never apply to a school you know you cannot afford unless you have a clear scholarship or aid strategy.

Step 5: Confirm Application Strategy

As your list comes together, check:
- Which schools offer Early Decision or Early Action
- Which schools track demonstrated interest
- Which schools require supplemental essays, interviews, portfolios, or any other additional information

Your list determines your workload. Choose wisely!

Step 6: Do a Final Reality Check

Before locking in your list, read it out loud and ask:

"Would I truly be happy at every school on this list?"

If the answer is yes, you are ready.

A balanced list doesn't just improve acceptance rates, it protects your confidence, your options, and your future.

Application Burnout

As a parent, it's tempting to push forward at full speed. After all, there's so much to do, and so much at stake. But here's something I share with every family:

Every student reaches a point of application burnout.

It's inevitable. There will come a time when your student doesn't want to hear about another essay, interview, or application portal. The Common App feels endless. Even conversations about college decisions can feel heavy.

And that's not because they're unmotivated.

It's because, at the same time, they're realizing something deeply personal: this is their final chapter of childhood. Their last homecoming. Their last football Friday. Their last season, performance, or rehearsal. The weight of those "lasts" settles in, and their tired, overworked minds need space.

This is where the right guidance matters most.

A pause is not a setback. A break is not falling behind. In fact, stepping back at the right moment allows students to return clearer, stronger, and better prepared for what comes next. The months ahead carry even more weight as I discuss in the upcoming chapters, students need energy and perspective to meet them well.

For parents, this is the season to trust the plan, trust the process, and allow your student to reset.

For students, it's time to hit the refresh button so they can move forward with confidence, clarity, and purpose.

And for families, it's a reminder that this journey is not about rushing to the finish line. It's about guiding your child thoughtfully through one of the most important transitions of their life.

TheAdmissionsEdge.com

If you found this book helpful, and I truly hope you did, there are additional resources that could be helpful, especially in the ever-changing college admissions world.

At my site www.TheAdmissionsEdge.com I publish new articles, some of which inspired this book as well as information that is either more timely or specific to unique circumstances.

You can find me on LinkedIn at www.linkedIn.com/in/colhart where I continually share more real-time information and quick updates.

Lastly, if you have any questions or are looking for dedicated help for your student, you can contact me at colleen@theadmissionsedge.com

Thank you for reading *The Admissions Edge, Your Path to College*. My hope is that this book helped bring clarity and confidence to a process that often feels confusing or overwhelming. College admissions are not about having everything figured out early or presenting a perfect version of yourself; it is about understanding your options, making thoughtful decisions, and finding environments where you can grow and thrive.

The process moves quickly, which is why focus matters more than trying to do everything at once. Students who take the time to understand their priorities, academically, personally, and socially, are more likely to feel satisfied with their college experience and comfortable with their choices. And there is no single path that works for everyone, only the one that fits you best.

If this book helped you see the process more clearly, ask better questions, or move forward with greater confidence, then it has done what it was meant to do. It was written to help you make choices that feel informed, intentional, and right for you.

www.ingramcontent.com/pod-product-compliance
Lightning Source LLC
Chambersburg PA
CBHW070248290326
41930CB00042B/2906